WEST LEYDEN ELEM

Y0-BNF-324

Jefferson-Lewis BOCES
CoSer 502
Coordinated Collection Development

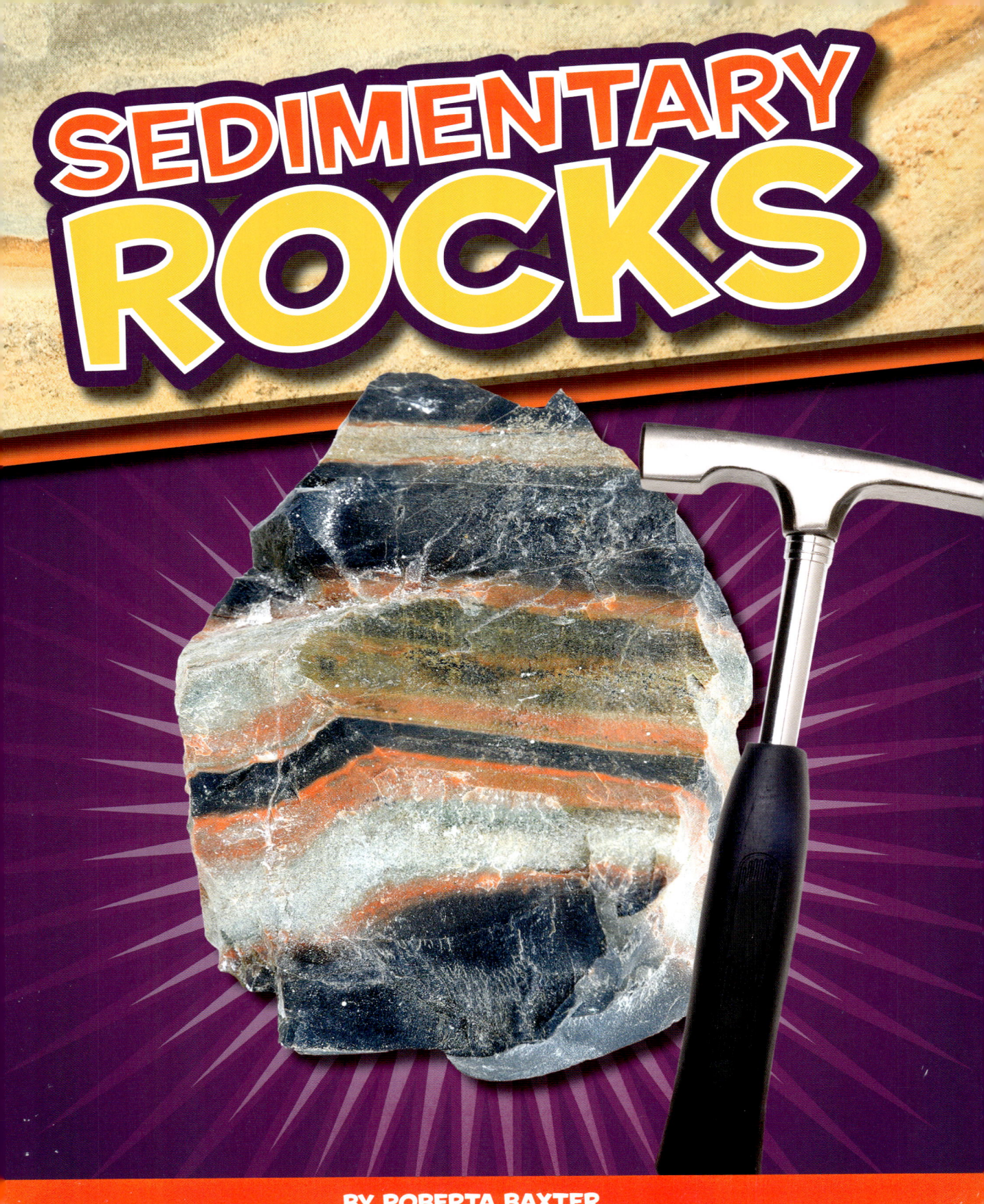

SEDIMENTARY ROCKS

BY ROBERTA BAXTER

Published by The Child's World®
1980 Lookout Drive • Mankato, MN 56003-1705
800-599-READ • www.childsworld.com

Acknowledgments
The Child's World®: Mary Swensen, Publishing Director
Red Line Editorial: Editorial direction and production
The Design Lab: Design

Design Element: Shutterstock Images
Photographs ©: Shutterstock Images, cover (top), cover (bottom left), cover (bottom right), 1 (top), 1 (bottom left), 1 (bottom right), 7, 9, 23; iStockphoto, 4, 5, 6, 8, 12, 18; NASA/JPL-Caltech/MSSS, 11; Santi Rodriguez/Shutterstock Images, 14; Rafal Cichawa/iStockphoto, 15; Tarek El Sombati/iStockphoto, 16; Nikitin Victor/Shutterstock Images, 19; Shank Ali/iStockphoto, 20; Przemyslaw Skibinski, 21

Copyright © 2017 by The Child's World®
All rights reserved. No part of this book may be reproduced or utilized in any form or by any means without written permission from the publisher.

ISBN 9781503808058
LCCN 2015958131

Printed in the United States of America
Mankato, MN
June, 2016
PA02305

ABOUT THE AUTHOR
Roberta Baxter has written more than 30 books for children and students of all ages. She writes most often about science and history. Baxter lives in Colorado.

CONTENTS

CHAPTER 1
What Are Sedimentary Rocks?...4

CHAPTER 2
Types of Sedimentary Rocks...8

CHAPTER 3
Canyons and Caves...12

CHAPTER 4
Fossils and Fuels...16

CHAPTER 5
How Sedimentary Rocks Change...19

GLOSSARY...22

TO LEARN MORE...23

INDEX...24

CHAPTER 1

What Are Sedimentary Rocks?

The white cliffs of Dover, England, are made of sedimentary rock.

You have probably seen pictures of the Grand Canyon. Huge ridges run along the Colorado River. Colorful rock layers span the canyon. Perhaps you have also seen the cliffs of Dover, England. The stiff white mounds rise up out of the ocean. Both of these sites get their beauty from **sedimentary rock**.

There are three types of rock on Earth. Sedimentary rock covers about 75% of the surface. It covers up to 90% of the ocean floor. The other types of rock, igneous and metamorphic, are often covered by sedimentary rock.

SANDSTONE TOOLS

Sandstone is a common sedimentary rock. Today, sandstone is often used in construction. People have been using sandstone for thousands of years. Prehistoric people used sandstone to make tools. These included axes and arrowheads.

Sedimentary rock is made from bits of sand, pebbles, and plant or animal matter. These tiny particles are called **sediments**. Often, wind and water carry the sediments. They can travel far. But they usually end up at the

Sediment includes bits of sand, as well as animal matter and small pebbles.

Sedimentary rock builds up in layers over time.

bottom of a lake or ocean. Over time, these sediments form layers. Pressure from the top layers squeezes the bottom layers. Over hundreds or thousands of years, the compressed bottom layers harden into rock.

The White Cliffs of Dover in England are one example. They formed underwater. Remains of sea algae combined with other sediments. The algae contained a white chemical. Over millions of years, the sediments became white rock. Meanwhile, the sea level dropped. Eventually, the cliffs were exposed.

The layers of sedimentary rock are called **strata**. They have a variety of colors. These colors come from different minerals. In the Grand Canyon, many of the rock layers contain iron. The iron gives the strata a red color.

Sedimentary rocks have some common traits. They contain layers. They are usually soft and crumbly. But the rocks can look very different from each other. Geologists study the traits of different sedimentary rocks. These traits show how the rocks formed.

Grand Canyon National Park includes sedimentary rock that is up to 1.8 billion years old.

CHAPTER 2

Types of Sedimentary Rocks

Rocks are made of more than one material. When you look closely at a rock, you can see the different parts. Sedimentary rocks include chunks and grains of different minerals.

One type of sedimentary rock is called **breccia**. Breccia contains large particles. The particles inside breccia have sharp edges. Most breccia rocks formed from pieces of earlier rocks. These rocks were shattered by ice or broken apart by volcanic action. Sandstone and limestone can form breccia.

Breccia includes layers of particles with sharp edges.

Conglomerate rocks contain a combination of pebbles and sand or clay.

Another type is a **conglomerate**. This type also has large particles. Conglomerate rocks have been tossed or dragged in water. The water grinds off the edges of the particles, making them smooth. Their large particles are heavier than sand or clay. These rocks may include pebble-sized rocks stuck together with sand or clay. The pebbles can still be seen in the rock.

Chemical rock is another type. It forms from evaporating or dripping water. The water contains dissolved minerals. As the water evaporates, the minerals form crystals. The crystals combine with other minerals to form rock.

Biological rock forms from remains of living things. When plants and animals die in a body of water, the remains sink to the bottom. The wind and water carry

AGES OF ROCKS IN THE GRAND CANYON

Geologists study rock layers to decide how old they are. The oldest layers are on the bottom. The newest layers are on the top. The rocks in the Grand Canyon have a variety of ages.

Kind of Rock	Approximate Age	Where the Rock Formed
Kaibab limestone	270 million years old	Shallow, warm sea full of sea animals
Coconino sandstone	275 million years old	Sand dunes
Hermit shale	280 million years old	Muddy water
Supai group (a variety of limestone, sandstone, and shale)	300 million years old	Sandy ocean floor
Redwall limestone	340 million years old	Warm sea
Bright angel shale	515 million years old	Muddy sea over the land

sediments into the water. Eventually, the sediment covers the remains. The layers are pressed together. They harden into rock. Coal is one type of biological rock.

The layers in sedimentary rock are not always even or equal in size. A flood can deposit a large amount of sediment in a lake or river. The sediment then forms a thick layer. During dry periods, thinner strips of sediment might form.

The NASA Curiosity rover has found conglomerate rocks on Mars.

Movements of Earth's plates can cause sedimentary rocks to tilt or bend. When the plates move against each other, they push up parts of the surface. Sometimes, the pressure folds the layers into strange shapes.

Sedimentary rocks do not only teach us about the history of Earth. They can also make stunning **landforms**, such as canyons and caves.

ROCKS ON MARS

The NASA rover *Curiosity* is exploring the surface of Mars. In 2012, *Curiosity* discovered conglomerate rocks. Pictures from the rover show rocks made up of pebbles stuck together. This discovery is strong evidence that Mars once had water. The particles were probably ground into smooth shapes as they moved in water. That's how pebbles become smooth on Earth.

CHAPTER 3

Canyons and Caves

The rocks at Canyonlands National Park in Utah eroded for millions of years, creating a variety of rock formations.

Have you ever seen the American Southwest? If so, you might have seen roads lined with canyons and caves. These canyons and caves are made from layers of sedimentary rock.

Canyons form over thousands of years. Sediment covered by a lake or ocean can be hundreds of feet thick. Rock forms from the sediment. Eventually, the water evaporates. The rock is exposed. Sometimes, rivers run across the rock. The water rubs a trench in the rock. The result is a canyon.

Canyons can also form in places without rivers. Rain seeps into cracks in the rock surface. When the water freezes, it expands. The ice forces the cracks open more. Over hundreds of years, rain carries off more of the rock. Eventually, a canyon is formed.

Water leaking into cracks in rock can start another process below the surface. Rainwater is slightly acidic. It can dissolve rock. As the rock dissolves, holes open up underground. The holes can grow larger and connect. They become a cave.

After a cave forms, water continues to drip through cracks. Each drop of water carries dissolved minerals from the rock. Inside the cave, this mixture forms **stalagmites** and **stalactites**.

Caves and canyons can vary greatly in size. Many are small. But some are vast and deep. Each year, millions of tourists go to see the Grand Canyon. This canyon is 5,699 feet (1,737 m) deep. The world's deepest canyon is in Peru. Cotahuasi Canyon is 11,003 feet (3,354 m) deep. That's more than 2 miles (3.2 km).

Many caves contain both stalagmites and stalactites.

These giant canyons can teach us about Earth's past. The Grand Canyon took millions of years to form. Geologists study the layers of sedimentary rock. They learn how old each layer is. They can also learn what the climate was like when each layer formed. The climate affects the texture of the rock.

Geologists are still making new discoveries about canyons. There are many canyons they haven't found yet. In 2013,

CARLSBAD CAVERNS

Carlsbad Caverns National Park is in southeastern New Mexico. An ocean once covered this area. Sediments on the seafloor hardened into a thick layer of limestone rock. The sea dried up. Rainwater dripped onto the rock. Eventually, openings began to form. Today, the caverns have at least 119 caves.

Cotahuasi Canyon in Peru is the deepest canyon in the world.

scientists discovered a vast canyon under an ice sheet in Greenland. It is about the same size as the Grand Canyon.

CHAPTER 4

Fossils and Fuels

Sedimentary rock can be beautiful. It can also be useful. Many animals live in caves made from sedimentary rock. The rock is useful to people, too. It teaches scientists about Earth's past. Fossils that form in the rock tell about past life on Earth. Sedimentary rock can also be used in fuel.

Biological rocks are made of plant and animal remains. Sometimes a plant or animal is buried by sediment. The body stays intact. As sediment presses down on it, the hard parts of the body remain. They turn into rock along with the sediment. The shape of the animal or plant is preserved in the rock. These traces are

Most fossils form in sedimentary rocks.

fossils. Fossils are found in a variety of types of rock. But almost all fossils form in sedimentary rock.

Several natural resources come from sedimentary rocks. These include gasoline and oil for cars. Coal is a type of sedimentary rock. Natural gas is also from sedimentary rocks. We use these resources to heat buildings. Coal, oil, and gas are called fossil fuels. This is because they come from plant and animal remains.

When the plants die, their remains stack up in layers. Other layers form on top. The bottom layers turn to rock under the weight. Heat from under Earth's crust cooks these layers. The heat and pressure make fossil fuels.

Different types of fossil fuels form in different areas. In most places, they turn into oil. The oil pools in cracks and holes in the rock. In very deep places

FOSSILS AT MONUMENTS

People can see fossils at national monuments. Florissant Fossil Beds National Monument is located in Colorado. Visitors to the monument can see fossils of plants and insects. About 1,700 species have been found. This monument also has petrified tree stumps. These trees turned into rock after they died. Dinosaur National Monument is in Utah and Colorado. This monument includes 1,500 dinosaur bones from sedimentary rock in the area.

underground, the remains turn into natural gas. Coal comes from swampy areas with many plants.

We use fossil fuels every day. These fuels help us travel. They heat our homes. However, Earth has a limited amount of fossil fuels. There are disadvantages to using fossil fuels, too. Some fuels, such as coal, can harm the environment. Scientists are looking for ways to limit the amount of fossil fuels we use.

Coal, a sedimentary rock, is used to heat buildings and to produce steel.

HOW FOSSIL FUELS FORM

Dead plant or animal matter forms a layer on the surface.

⬇

Other layers of sediments form on top.

⬇

The lower layers press together and turn into rock.

⬇

Heat and pressure transform plant or animal matter into fossil fuels.

CHAPTER 5

How Sedimentary Rocks Change

Sedimentary rocks are all around us. But they do not always remain sedimentary rocks. Over hundreds or thousands of years, they change into other types of rocks.

One of these types is **metamorphic rock**. The name *metamorphic* comes from *metamorphosis*, which means "change." As sedimentary rocks are pushed lower into

Heat and pressure can transform sedimentary rock into metamorphic rock.

the Earth's crust, they are under great pressure and heat. Eventually, they become metamorphic rocks. For example, limestone is a type of sedimentary rock. Heat and pressure can change it into marble. Marble is a type of metamorphic rock.

Sedimentary rocks can also change into **igneous rock**. If sedimentary rock is pressed down below Earth's crust, it can melt. The melted rock flows out as magma, then cools. It becomes igneous rock. When sedimentary rock becomes another type of rock, only the structure changes. The same minerals make up the rock.

These changes are part of the rock cycle. Over many years, rock transforms. Sedimentary rock becomes igneous or metamorphic rock. Then, as time passes, the rock breaks apart. Wind and water cause **erosion**. Bits of broken rock combine with other sediments. They become sedimentary rock again.

Igneous rocks can form from melted sedimentary rock.

Talampaya National Park in La Rioja, Argentina, features sandstone rock formations.

Sedimentary rocks are useful and beautiful. We see them all around us. We study fossils found in them. Materials such as oil are made from sedimentary rocks. The world would be very different without sedimentary rocks.

GLOSSARY

breccia *(BRECH-ee-uh)* Breccia is a type of rock made up of sharp-edged particles. The breccia had flakes of gray with sharp edges.

conglomerate *(kun-GLOM-er-it)* A conglomerate is a rock made up of rounded particles. The conglomerate contained round brown pebbles.

erosion *(i-ROH-zhun)* During erosion, natural forces carry away bits of worn-down rock. Water, glaciers, and wind can all cause erosion.

igneous rock *(IG-nee-us ROK)* Igneous rock is formed from melted magma or lava. Magma hardens into igneous rock.

landforms *(LAND-formz)* Landforms are natural parts of Earth's surface. Some landforms include canyons and caves.

metamorphic rock *(met-uh-MOR-fik ROK)* Metamorphic rock is transformed igneous or sedimentary rock. Heat or pressure can cause metamorphic rock to form.

sedimentary rock *(sed-uh-MEN-tuh-ree ROK)* Sedimentary rock forms from sediment carried by water or air. Often, sedimentary rock forms near seas or lakes.

sediments *(SED-uh-mints)* Sediments are bits of sand, animal matter, and plant remains. Over many years, sediments can gather and harden into rock.

stalactites *(stuh-LAK-tites)* Stalactites are formations that hang from the ceiling of a cave. Stalactites form from water and minerals.

stalagmites *(stuh-LAG-mites)* Stalagmites are formed from water dripping onto the floor of a cave. Stalagmites often have rounded tips.

strata *(STRAH-tuh)* Strata are layers of a material. Over the years, rock forms strata that show how the rock has changed.

TO LEARN MORE

IN THE LIBRARY

Dee, Willa. **Unearthing Sedimentary Rocks**. New York: PowerKids, 2014.

O'Neal, Claire. **A Project Guide to Rocks and Minerals**. Hockessin, DE: Mitchell Lane, 2011.

Rau, Dana Meachen. **Real World Science: Rocks and Minerals**. Ann Arbor, MI: Cherry Lake, 2009.

Tomecek, Steve. **Everything Rocks and Minerals**. Washington, DC: National Geographic, 2010.

ON THE WEB

Visit our Web site for links about sedimentary rocks: **childsworld.com/links**

Note to Parents, Teachers, and Librarians: We routinely verify our Web links to make sure they are safe and active sites. So encourage your readers to check them out!

23

INDEX

algae, 6
animals, 5, 9, 10, 16, 17, 18

biological rock, 9, 10, 16
breccia, 8

Carlsbad Caverns, 14
caves, 11, 12-14, 16
chemical rock, 6, 9
coal, 10, 17, 18
conglomerate rock, 9, 11
Cotahuasi Canyon, 13, 15
crystals, 9
Curiosity rover, 11

dinosaurs, 17
Dover, England, 4, 6

erosion, 20

Florissant Fossil Beds, 17
fossils, 16-18, 21
fuel, 16-18

gas, 17, 18
Grand Canyon, 4, 7, 10, 13, 14, 15
Greenland, 15

igneous rock, 5, 20

limestone, 8, 10, 14, 20

marble, 20
Mars, 11
metamorphic rock, 5, 19-20
minerals, 7, 8, 9, 13, 20

oil, 17, 21

Peru, 13, 15
plants, 5, 9, 16-18
pressure, 6, 11, 17, 18, 19, 20

sandstone, 5, 8, 10, 21
stalactites, 13, 14
stalagmites, 13, 14
strata, 7